EMERALDS
carved with thoughts

कुछ पन्ने विचारों से तराशे हुए

**A Poetic Saga by
Ashish Sharma**

English Translation by
Ashish Sharma & Yogita Sharma

First published in 2019 by

Becomeshakespeare.com

Wordit Content Design & Editing Services Pvt Ltd
Unit - 26, Building A -1, Nr Wadala RTO,
Wadala (East), Mumbai 400037, India
T: +91 8080226699

The information in this book is true & complete to the best of our knowledge as on or before 31st May' 2019. The content is purely the poet's opinion & not anti or pro to any individual in specific or any political party in specific or any government / any administration / any organisation etc. in specific. All recommendations (if any) are made without guarantee on part of author or translator or publisher. The author, translator & publisher disclaim any liability in connection with the use of this information.

©

ISBN - 978-93-88573-30-6

The First Copy of the Book
is Presented
To
"The Almighty" – Sri Markandey Rishi Ji

प्रथम प्रति भगवान श्री मार्कण्डेय ऋषि जी के चरणों में समर्पित

This Book is Dedicated
To
Our Loving Parents
Prof.Harinder Sharma & Mrs.Uttra Sharma
MWO(Retd) Mr. Som Nath Kapil & Mrs. Premlata Kapil

May the Kind God give them a long life -

Ashish & Yogita

यह पुस्तक हमारे माता.पिता को समर्पित है, परमात्मा उन्हें दीर्घायु प्रदान करे, यही हमारी कामना है - आशीष और योगिता

Prof.Harinder Sharma &
Mrs.Uttra Sharma

MWO(Retd) Mr. Som Nath Kapil &
Mrs. Premlata Kapil

Acknowledgements

First of all, thank you from the bottom of my heart for appreciating my last two publications "PEARLS from the Ocean of Heart" – "कुछ मोती दिल के सागर से" and "DIAMONDS from the Mine of Mind – "कुछ हीरे मन की खान से". This time, I present to you, "EMERALDS carved with thoughts" – "कुछ पन्ने विचारों से तराशे हुए", which, like my last two books, is a Poetic Passion, encompassing various global issues, societal evils, some events from history and some moments of my life.

My wife Yogita and I feel blessed & honoured that Mrs. Savita Bhatti released my last two books and with the grace of God this book will also be released by her. We thank her from the bottom of our hearts for all the encouragement and blessings we have received from her.

This time, I really feel humbly proud that I could write in honour of some Great Personalities, whose lives have been a source of inspiration for millions. In this book, you would find poems on some Great Personalities like the Dynamic Hon'ble Prime Minister of India Shri. Narendra Modi, Hon'ble Former Prime Minister of India & Great Poet Late Shri. Atal Bihari Vajpayee, the King of meaningful comedy Late Shri. Jaspal Bhatti, Great philanthropist & Hon'ble founder of HSA Group Late Mr. Hayel Saeed Anam (HSA) & My Loving Parents Prof. Harinder Sharma & Mrs.Uttra Sharma.

Year 2019-2020 is a great year which will be known as 70th

year for the Strong Friendship between the two Great Nations – India & Indonesia. I am glad, that to commemorate this Golden moment, I could write a Poem on the friendship of these two great nations & publish in this book.

I would like to thank my lovely wife, Yogita (Meenu), who has been a source of inspiration all through life. During the making of all the three books, her help & support has been immense. Thank you for all the English translation and corrections. I would also like to thank our lovely daughter, Apurva (Aru) & dashing son, Abhilaksh (Lakshi); they both have been very supportive, affectionate and loving children. They played a great role in suggesting some concepts & corrections, as always.

My warm regards and thanks to my parents – Prof. Harinder Sharma & Mrs. Uttra Sharma, who always have been source of blessings, inspiration & encouragement. I would also like to convey my warm regards and thanks to my parents-in-law – MWO (Retd.) S.N. Kapil & Mrs. Prem Lata Kapil for all the encouragement and support. Blessings from parents are always divine blessings.

My wife and I would like to convey our humble thanks & best regards to Mr. Fouad Hayel Saeed Anam & Mr. Salah A.H. Saeed for all support and encouragement. They are great human beings and great employers. We humbly thank them for everything.

With heavy heart my thanks to Late Sh. Kesar Das (Uncle *ji*) – Former President, Shri Markandeshwar Mandir Sabha, Shahbad Markandey and Former General Secretary, Managing Committee M.N. College, Shahbad Markandey for all his blessings. We lost him, may the Kind God give peace to his soul.

I would also like to thank Dr. Harjit Singh (Uncle *ji*) – a noted Punjabi poet for being an inspiration. His valuable inputs are always appreciated and helped me to improve my writing. He is a teacher with teachings for life, blessed to have you in my life.

I would like to thank my brother, Akshay, and his wife, Salja for being a good support in life always. Thanks to my sisters-in-law Pratibha Dutta, Lipika Bawani, Parul and brothers-in-law Kuber Dutta, Maulik Bawani and our loving Nikhil (Shanu).

I would like to convey my thanks & regards to Pooja Dutt & Sameer Ambildhok of Wordit, who played a major role my third book and making the concept become reality. My sincere thanks to Anagha Bailur for her great editing job. Thanks to them, that we are able to present these selected Pearls, Diamonds & Emeralds in the form of poems to the society.

My sincere thanks to cover designers, page setting teams, printers & all others associated with making of the book. People behind the scene always play an important role & they deserve a Big Thanks.

I would like to sincerely thank all my respected uncles, respected aunties, my cousins, my sisters-in-law, my brothers-in-law, all my friends and near & dear ones for the blessings, support & cooperation all along the journey of life.

Finally, my love to our loving kids who fill my life with Enthusiasm, Passion & Inspiration with their Love & Affection. Live Long My Loveable Gems – Apurva (Aru), Abhinav (Avi), Abhilaksh (Lakshi), Annanya (Nannu) & our Laddu & Chamcham – Riyan & Vivan.

At the end, I would just like to say that our relationships, dreams, ambitions, thoughts, goals, purposes, values, the good

& bad, happy & sorrow moments of life, all are precious gems like DIAMONDS, EMERALDS & PEARLS. Life is nothing but a big collection of all these.

पढ़ते रहिए, बढ़ते रहिए, खुश रहिए ☺

KEEP READING, KEEP MOVING, STAY HAPPY ☺

EMERALDS
carved with thoughts

"कुछ पन्ने विचारों से तराशे हुए"

A Poetic Saga by Ashish Sharma

Translated to English
with

My Better Half

Dear Readers,

After "PEARLS from the Ocean of Heart"- "कुछ मोती दिल के सागर से" & "DIAMONDS from the Mine of Mind" - "कुछ हीरे मन की खान से", we are back with "EMERALDS carved with thoughts" - "कुछ पन्ने विचारों से तराशे हुए".

We have chosen again to translate Hindi Poems to English to remove the language barrier, because we wanted everyone (Indian & Otherwise) to enjoy these equally & to share our thoughts. We are afraid some of it may get lost in translation, however we have done our best to capture the essence of Hindi poems in English.

We hope you would like these Poems & appreciate the efforts.

Enjoy Reading !!

Ashish & Yogita Sharma

विषय सूचि

Contents

Hon'ble Prime Minister of India Shree Narendra Modi

1

कर्म–योगी नरेंद्र मोदी

यह कविता, भारत के प्रधानमंत्री श्री नरेन्द्र मोदी जी के व्यक्तित्व एवं उनकी उपलब्धियों पर आधारित है। यह कविता 30 मई 2018 को उनके जकारता, इंडोनेशिया आगमन पर उनके सम्मान में लिखी गई। कविता में मोदी जी की तुलना सूर्य से की गई है। जैसे सूर्य के प्रकाश से काले बादल छँट जाते हैं, ऐसे ही उनका प्रकाश भारत एवं विश्व को ऐसे ही रौशन करता रहे, यही कामना है।

जहाँ धरती अम्बर हैं मिलते,
वहाँ अद्भुत लाली छाई है,
ओ काले बादल रस्ता दो,
सूरज की सवारी आई है।

किरणों की अद्भुत आभा से,
भारत का कण–कण जागा है,
हर जन–जन में है जोश भरा,
उमंग नई लहराई है।

"नमो–नमो" के शँखनाद से,
मधुर ध्वनि है गूँज उठी,
हर गाँव–शहर बिजली पहुँची,
"उज्ज्वला" क्रांति आई है।

हर ओर विकास की धार बही,
उन्नत भारत की साख बढ़ी,
प्रगति–रथ प्रगति–पथ दौड़े,
समृद्धि घर–घर में आई है।

योग–पताका विश्व पटल पर,
तुमने ही फहराया है,
रोग योग से भाग रहे,
स्वास्थ्य की सरिता बहाई है।

"स्वच्छ हिंद (भारत)" नन्हें बचपन को सींच रहा,
नव–भारत नव–अवसर नित–नित खोज रहा,
हर बेटी को अब अपना अधिकार मिला,
अब सपनों ने छू ली हर ऊंचाई है।

नरसिंह "मोदी" की दहाड़ से,
दुश्मन अब थर–थर काँप रहा,
चिंतित–विचलित वो भांप रहा,
भारत से अब करनी नहीं लड़ाई है।

"नरेन्द्र" बसा हर भारतवासी के मन में,
नई साधना नई चेतना जन–जन में,
नव–स्वरूप का नव–भारत अवतरित हुआ,
हर जन–जन की होती अब सुनवाई है।

सूरज से कर्म–योगी बन कर,
नित अपना तेज हो बाँट रहे,
अपनी ऊर्जा की शक्ति से,
हर हृदय–मशाल जलाई है।

ओ काले बादल रस्ता दो,
सूरज की सवारी आई है।

I

Karma-Yogi Narendra Modi

This Poem is based on the personality & achievements of The Prime Minister of India Mr. Narendra Modi. The poem was written in his honour, on his arrival at Jakarta, Indonesia on 30 May 2018. Mr.Modi has been compared with The Sun, in the poem. As the black clouds part away from the sunlight, we wish that Mr. Modi's aura keeps brightening India & the World with its shine.

Where the earth & the sky meet (at the Horizon),The unique red vibrance is high,
O! Black clouds give way,
The Sun comes with its convey (glory).

With the unique splendor of rays,
India has waken up every inch & ways,
The masses are filled with passion,
Rippling are new waves of enthusiasm.

With the sacred chants of "NAMO-NAMO",
Everywhere spreads a pleasant melody,
Electrification has reached every village & city,
There is an "UJJWALA" revolution.

There is development everywhere,
Credibility of developed India grew manifolds,
The chariot of progress is rolling fast on path of progress,
There is prosperity in every home.

Only You have unfurled
Flag of Yoga in the world,
With Yoga, Diseases are curing,
And River of health is flowing...

"Clean India" is nurturing the childhood,
New India is exploring new opportunities,
Every girl now gets her rights,
Now the dreams are touching the heights.

With the roar of Lion Man "MODI",
The enemy is shivering in fear,
And the worried-distracted are guessing,
Now it (enemy) cannot enter in a war with India.

"Narendra" lives in the heart of every Indian,
There is new awakening in the masses,
The New India with new face has emerged,
Now voice of everybody is heard.

Like "Karm-Yogi" as The Sun,
You are spreading your glow,
With the power of your passion,
You have lightened up the torch in every heart.

O! Black clouds give way,
The Sun comes with its convey (glory).

2

ये धरा – वसुंधरा

यह कविता हमारी धरती का व्याख्यान करती है। हमारी पृथ्वी में न जाने कितने पर्वत, नदियाँ, सागर और जंगल समाए हैं। हमारी ये धरा सबका संतुलन बना घूमती है और हमें जीवन प्रदान करती है। कविता अंत में पृथ्वी की समस्त मानवजाति को प्रेरित करती है कि हम सब इसको स्वच्छ एवं सुंदर बनाए रखने का प्रण करें।

ये धरा – वसुंधरा,
अपने में समाए है,
परबत, दरिया, सहरा, जंगल, झरने,
जाने क्या–क्या ....
ये धरा – वसुंधरा।

ये ब्रह्मांड, है प्रचंड,
इसमें विचरे ये धरा,
घूमे ही जाए है,
अपनी ही चाल से,
अपने ही वेग से,
बिना कहीं रुके हुए,
बिना कहीं थके हुए,
करती है सूरज की परिक्रमा।

परबतों की श्रृंखला आसमां को चूमतीं,
पुष्पों से लदी वादियाँ लह–लहा के झूमतीं,
झर–झर चाँदी से बहते झरने,
जीवन–दायक शीतल नदियाँ,
जाशीले महासागर कहीं उफान मारते,
ज्वालामुखी दहकते अंगारे उछालते,
चादर सफ़ेद रंग की बर्फ़ है ओढ़ा रही,
कहीं तपते रेगिस्तान को एक बदली चिढ़ा रही।

नील वर्ण सागर,
हरा वनस्पति,
श्वेत रंग बर्फ़ानी,
रंग भूरा मिट्टी,
सुशोभित इन वर्णों से,
धरा ये पटराणी,
बन के अंगरक्षक,
परिमंडल करता चंद्रमा।

जननी है सबकी ये धरा–मातेश्वरी वसुंधरा,
इसका हृदय विशाल करूणा–भाव से भरा हुआ,
इसकी रक्षा–इसकी स्वच्छता, कर्तव्य है हर प्राणी का,
इसकी आन–इसकी शान – बरक़रार रखना – ये शंखनाद गूँजता,
जो समझे न हम आज मोल इस अमूल्य देन का,
कोसेंगी सोच को हमारी आने वाली पीढ़ियाँ,
हो रक्त–सिंचित भाव ये जगत के हर प्राणी में,
प्रण है हमारा हे धरा ! हर प्रयत्न कर के रखेंगे तेरी सुंदरता।

ये धरा – वसुंधरा,
अपने में समाए है,
परबत, दरया, सहरा, जंगल, झरने,
जाने क्या–क्या...
ये धरा – वसुंधरा।

2

The Earth

This poem praises our planet, Earth. Our Earth has so many mountains, rivers, seas & forests. It keeps rotating, maintaining the balance among all these elements & gives us life. In the end, the poem motivates the whole of mankind to take a pledge to keep the earth clean & beautiful.

The Earth - Vasundhara(A name of earth in Hindi)
has contained in herself,
Mountains, rivers, deserts, woods, waterfalls,
And don't know what all ....
The Earth – Vasundhara.

This universe is massive,
The earth moves in this,
it keeps moving,
with its style,
with its pace,
without stopping,
without tiring,
it circles around the sun.

The mountain ranges kiss the sky,
The flower laden valleys flaunt in style,
The waterfalls flow like silver stream,
The vitalizing rivers,
The passionate oceans are pouncing,
The volcanoes are steaming & springing blaze,
The ice is spreading like a white sheet,
A small cloud is teasing some desert somewhere.

The blue colour of ocean,
The green colour of vegetation,
The white colour of snow,
The brown colour of soil,
The queen earth is adorned with,
these colours,
Acting as bodyguard,
The moon circles around the earth.

This earth is our mother,
It's heart is large & filled with kindness,
The protection & cleanliness of earth is every human's
responsibility,
There is a roaring slogan to keep its dignity & honour,
If we don't understand today the value of this priceless boon,
We will be cursed by the generations to come,
Let there be a thought in the blood of each human of the
world,
O Earth ! It is our promise that we will keep you clean
with all efforts.

The Earth - Vasundhara
has contained in itself,
Mountains, rivers, deserts, woods, waterfalls,
And don't know what all...
The Earth - Vasundhara

Hon'ble Former Prime Minister of India, Late Shree Atal Bihari Vajpayee.

3

अटल सत्य को अटल पुरुष ने पार किया

यह कविता भारत के भूतपूर्व प्रधानमंत्री स्व. श्री अटल बिहारी वाजपेयी के सम्मान में लिखी गई है। वे 16 अगस्त 2018 को सदा के लिए हमें छोड़ कर अनंत यात्रा पर चले गए। उनका जीवन हम सब के लिए प्रेरणास्रोत है और सदैव रहेगा। उनके संदेश हमेशा भारत की आने वाली पीढ़ियों को प्रेरित करते रहेंगे।

अटल सत्य को अटल पुरुष ने पार किया,
अटल पुरुष जाते–जाते भी अटल ज्ञान है बाँट गया –

अटल पुरुष बोला – भारत से,
अटल इरादे से बढ़ना,
आँख लगा के विश्व देखता,
नभ के तारों को छू लेना।

अटल पुरुष बोला हिंद–प्रचंड–युवा–शक्ति से,
ऐ भारत के उज्जवल भविष्य,
अटल उम्मीद करता हूँ तुमसे,
अटल लक्ष्य अर्जित करना।

अटल पुरुष बोला – हिंद के पहरेदारों से,
अटल प्रतिज्ञा–अटल इरादा,
भारत माँ की आन का सदक़ा,
अटल विजय हासिल करना।

अटल पुरुष बोला – भारत की सरकारों से,
अटल शक्ति–अटल ऊर्जा,
कण–कण में संचालित करना,
इक नया हिंद निर्मित करना।

अटल पुरुष बोला – भारत के विद्वानों से,
आज तुम्हारे कंधे पे ज़िम्मा इक छोड़ के जाता हूँ
विशाल हृदय और अटल निश्चय से,
नव पीढ़ी को सिंचित करना।

अटल पुरुष बोला – भारत के कृषि किसानों से,
ताक़त तुम में मिट्टी को सोना कर दो,
तुमसे रोशन ये गुलशन है,
तुम इसको सदा हरा रखना।

अटल पुरुष बोला – भारतमाता से,
अटल वचन देता हूँ तुमको,
लौट के फिर मैं आऊँगा,
ऐ मातृभूमि ! फिर से तेरी सेवा में रम जाऊँगा।

अटल सत्य को अटल पुरुष ने पार किया...

3.

The Firm (Atal) Man has achieved
the sacrosanct truth

This poem was written in the honour of the former Prime Minister of India, Late Shree Atal Bihari Vajpayee. He left all of us for his heavenly abode on 16 August 2018. His life has been and will continue to remain a source of inspiration for all of us, forever. His messages will keep on inspiring future generations to come.

The Firm (Atal) Man has achieved a sacrosanct truth,
The Firm Man has spread the sacrosanct knowledge before leaving -

The Firm man addressed to India,
March with a firm determination,
The world is watching you carefully,
You touch the stars in the sky (Grow High context).

The Firm Man addressed to the massive youth power of India,
O ! The bright future of India,
I have a firm expectation from you,
You achieve the firm goals.

The Firm Man addressed to the soldiers of India,
with steadfast commitment & firm determination,
for the dignity of Mother India,
You achieve the firm victory.

The Firm Man addressed to the Governments of India,
channeling in every inch of India,
the steadfast power & firm energy,
build a New India.

The Firm Man addressed to the scholars of India,
I am going, leaving a responsibility on your shoulders
today,
with a large heart & firm determination,
nurture the new generation.

The Firm Man addressed to the farmers of India,
You have the power to grow gold from this soil,
with you only this garden (India) is flourishing,
You always keep it green.

The Firm Man addressed to The Mother India,
I give you a firm promise,
I will come back,
O Mother Land ! I will again dedicate myself for your
service.

The Firm (Atal) Man has achieved the sacrosanct truth...

4.

बेबाक़ क़लम

यह कविता मेरी अंतरात्मा की आवाज़ है, जो मुझसे ये पूछ रही है कि मैं क्यूँ लिखता हूँ ? मेरा प्रयास है कि मैं जो भी लिखूँ, वो पढ़ने वालों के दिल को छू जाए और उनकी सोच का रुख़ मोड़ दे। कविता अंत में यह संदेश देती है कि, मैं बेबाक और बेख़ौफ़ होकर पूरे ज़ोर से बेबाक क़लम से सच्ची बात लिखूँ।

इक दिन बैठा सोच रहा था,
दिल की बात टटोल रहा था,
कल और आज को जोड़ रहा था,
लम्हों में सपने घोल रहा था,
एक सफ़ेद से पन्ने पर,
शब्दों के रत्न बटोर रहा था,
और ! गहरी सोच की वादी से,
एक सवाल ने दस्तक दी,
कि मैं क्यूँ लिखता हूँ ?
जी हाँ ! मैं क्यूँ लिखता हूँ !?
जब पूछा अपने–आप से,
पाया जवाब – जो मैं यूँ कहता हूँ –
लिखूँ तो ऐसा, कि पढ़ने वालों पे छाप छोड़ जाऊँ,
कहूँ तो ऐसा, कि सुनने वालों का रुख़ मोड़ जाऊँ,
जब भी पूछता हूँ ख़ुद से, कि मैं क्यूँ लिखता हूँ !?
यही जवाब भीतर से पाता हूँ हरसू,
लिखूँ दिल से, कि दिलों को छू जाऊँ।

कुछ लिखूँ आज की बात पे,
कुछ दुनिया के हालात पे,
कुछ सिस्के से जज़्बात पे,
कुछ हम पे, कुछ आप पे।

कुछ लिखूँ बीती तारीख़ पे,
कुछ होने वाले अहसास पे,
कुछ उजले कल की सोच पे,
कुछ धरती, सागर और मेघ पे।

कुछ लिखूँ कि हालात बदल जाएँ,
कुछ लिखूँ कि तल्ख़ी घट जाए,
कुछ लिखूँ कि रूहे—सुकूँ मिले,
कुछ लिखूँ अमन की राह पे।

कुछ लिखूँ कि लहू सफ़ेद न हो,
और ऊँच—नीच का भेद न हो,
कुछ लिखूँ कि ग़ैरत जग जाए,
मरता ज़मीर फिर जी जाए।

कुछ लिखूँ कि नया सवेरा हो,
जो उजला और सुनहरा हो,
और व्योम के मस्तक पर नव—सूरज,
उज्जवल भविष्य ले ठहरा हो।

बेबाक़ लिखूँ, निःस्वार्थ लिखूँ
जो सच में है, वो बात लिखूँ
बेख़ौफ़ लिखूँ, पुरज़ोर लिखूँ,
"बेबाक़ क़लम" के साथ लिखूँ।

4.

The Fearless Pen

This poem is the voice of my self-conscious, asking me, 'Why do I write'? I always try that whatever I write should touch the heart of its readers & change their way of thinking. In the end, the poem gives the message that I write the truth strongly with a Fearless Pen, without any fear.

One fine day, I was thinking,
was trying to find the thoughts of my heart,
was trying to connect the present & the past,
was mixing dreams in the moments,
was securing (scribbling) some gems of words,
on a white paper,
And suddenly, from the valley of dense thoughts,
one question knocked,
that why do I write!?
When I asked myself,
I got this answer, which I say as below -
I should write in such a way, that it leaves an impression
on the readers,
I should say such, that it changes the way of thinking of
the listeners,

Whenever I ask from self, that why do I write!?,
I always get this answer from my inner conscious, that I
must write with my heart, so that it touches the hearts of
the Readers.

I write something on today's thoughts,
Something on condition of the world,
Something on sobbing sentiments,
Something on you & us.

I write something on the past,
Something on the future Intuitions,
Something on the thoughts of bright future,
Something on the earth, oceans & clouds.

I write something to change the situations,
I write something to reduce the tensions,
I write something to soothe the soul,
I write something for peace.

I write something that the blood doesn't turn white (in
the context of compromising the values),
And there is no discrimination on upper & lower castes,
I write something that self-dignity awakes,
and the dying self-conscious lives again.

I write something that there is a new morning (new
beginning),
which is brighter & golden,
and the new sun on the forehead of the sky,
is shining with bright future.

I write without fear unselfishly,
I write the truth,
I write with all power fearlessly,
I write with "Fearless Pen".

The King of meaningful comedy Late Mr. Jaspal Bhatti

5.

"जसपाल जी" तुस्सी ग्रेट हो ...

यह कविता सार्थक कॉमेडी के बेताज बादशाह श्री जसपाल भट्टी जी के सार्थक व्यंग्य पर आधारित है। वे अपने व्यंग्य से समाज की बुराइयों से लड़ते थे। अंत में कविता ये संदेश देती है कि भले ही आज जसपालजी हमारे बीच न हों, पर उनके सार्थक हास्यपूर्ण व्यंग्य वाले संदेश सदैव सब को प्रेरित करते रहेंगे। मैं यह मानता हूँ कि जिनकी रचनाएँ आज भी "उलटा–पुलटा" कर के सब सीधा कर देती हैं और जो भविष्य को सुधारने की क्षमता रखते हैं, उन "जसपाल जी" पर भूतकाल में लिखना उचित नहीं, इसी लिए मैंने कविता को वर्तमान काल में लिखा है। "जसपाल जी" तुस्सी ग्रेट हो...

तुम "उलटा पुलटा" कर के भी,
सब कुछ सीधा कर देते हो,
कौन कहे तुम चले गए,
तुम दिलों में ज़िंदा रहते हो।

मंहगाई की आवाज़ उठा,
कभी बिजली कट पे लड़ते हो,
और "पावर कट" का व्यंग्य बना,
सरकार जगाया करते हो।

कभी पहन के चोगा बाबा का,
अंधविश्वासों से लड़ते हो,

"माहौल ठीक है" चल–चित्र से,
पुलिस का चित्रण करते हो।

तुम गाडी (car) के आगे लगा के घोड़ा,
सरपट दौड़ा करते हो,
पेट्रोल के बढ़ते दामों पर,
नकेल कसा तुम करते हो।

हँसी–हँसी और खेल–खेल में,
बात बड़ी समझाते हो,
कभी बना कार्टून नेता का,
सच्ची बात बताते हो।

"शाहजी की एडवाईस" से,
सब काम सँवारा करते हो,
"जीजा जी" के "फ़्लोप शो" से
सिस्टम को झंझोरा करते हो।

कविता पढ़ पाठक सोचेंगे,
ओ "शर्मा जी" चकराए हो !?
"जसपालजी" तो चले गए,
तुम पूरी कविता में वर्तमान दिखाए हो !?

सुन लो बंधू उत्तर मेरा,
जो भी सिस्टम से लड़ता है,
व्यंग्य या लेखन–चित्रों से या ऊँचे–ऊँचे नारों से,
सब में "भट्टी" ही दिखता है।

वो आज भी जन–जन के मन में,
मशाल जला कर जीता है,
भूत–काल में लिखूँ क्यूँ उस पर,
जो भविष्य को लिखता है।

"जसपाल जी" तुस्सी ग्रेट हो...

5

"Jaspal ji" You are Great ...

This poem is based on the satires of the king of meaningful comedy Mr.Jaspal Bhatti. He used to fight the evils of society with his satires. In the end, the poem gives the message that although Mr. Jaspal Bhatti is not among us today, his meaningful satirical comedy will keep on inspiring all, always. I believe that, he, whose creations have the capability of bending things to make them straight with "Ulta-Pulta" (upside down) & he, who has the capacity to brighten the future, such a personality is none other than - Jaspal Ji, it will not be appropriate at all, to write in his memory in the past tense, and so I have written the whole poem in the present tense. "Jaspal Ji, You are Great..."

Even with upside down,
You bend the things straight,
Who can say that you have gone,
You live in the hearts (of millions).

Raising a word against inflation,
You fight against electric cuts,
and making a satire on "Power Cut",
You wake up the government.

Sometimes wearing the costumes of a monk,
You fight with superstitions,
with the movie "Mahaul Theek Hai",
You portrayed the police.

You, by carting a horse with car,
move in a style & pace,
and on the rising prices of petrol,
You control with your satire.

You teach a big meaning,
in just a casual laughter,
Sometimes making the cartoons of political leaders,
You say the truth.

With "Shah ji ki advice",
You always give solutions,
With "Jija ji" & "Flop Show",
You shake the system.

After reading this poem, readers would think,
O Mr.Sharma (Me as Poet) have you gone crazy !?
"Jaspal Ji" have already gone,
And you (Me as Poet) have written whole poem in present
tense !?

My friends (readers), Listen my answer,
The One who fights with the system,
with satire or writing or paintings or with roaring slogans,
I see "Bhatti" (Jaspal Bhatti) in everyone (As source of
inspiration).

He lives even today, in the hearts of the masses,
by enlightening the torch (of revolution),
Why should I write on him in the past tense,
who writes the future.

"Jaspal ji" You are Great...

6

मेरा ज़िद्दी जज़्बा

यह कविता उन सभी नकारात्मक सोच रखने वालों के लिए है, जो अपनी नकारात्मक सोच से अच्छे लोगों के लिए मुश्किलें पैदा करते हैं। ऐसे लोगों को किसी दूसरे को कम नहीं आँकना चाहिए। कविता किसी व्यक्ति विशेष पर नहीं बल्कि नकारात्मक सोच पर बेबाक़ क़लम से एक चेतावनी है। हम अपने जज़्बे और पुरज़ोर सकारात्मक ताक़त से ऐसी नकारात्मक सोच का मुक़ाबला कर सकते हैं।

वो जो जलते हैं मेरी ऊँचाइयों को देख कर,
मेरी दुआ है, ख़ुदा बक़्श दे उनको भी एक पंखों का जोड़ा।

मेरी शक़्सीयत है कि चलूँ साथ दुश्मनों के भी,
पर वक़्त आने पे मालूम है बख़ूबी अकेले भी चलना।

वक़्त की फ़ितरत है कि वक़्त बदल जाता है,
मेरी फ़ितरत नहीं बदलते वक़्त में रंग बदलना।

वो जो गिरगिट की तरह बदलते हैं रंग अक्सर,
ऐसे चंद यारों से सीख़ लिया मैंने भी इन्सान को पढ़ना।

ना समझो महज़ मुझको एक उड़ता धूल का क़तरा,
हुनर है क़तरा—क़तरा जोड़ के सैलाब बन जाना।

छोड़ दो ये हसरतें कि क़ैद कर लोगे मुझे,
ये ज़िद्दी जज़्बा है मेरा नहीं कोई पालतू घोड़ा।

जो करते हैं मुझे बर्बाद करने की कड़ी साज़िश,
नहीं मालूम उनको उस खुदा का क़हर बरसाना।

खुश होते हो मुझे तुम झोंक कर जलते अंगारों में,
हमें मालूम है शोलों में तप के कुंदन हो जाना।

मेरे जज़्बात से खेलो, ये हक़ तुमको कभी न था,
मेरी चुप्पी में शोले हैं, हो जो हिम्मत कभी तुम आज़मा लेना।

तुम्हारी हैसियत होगी, मेरे पंखों को तुम कुतरो,
मेरे जज़्बों में ताक़त है कि अपने दम पे उड़ जाना।

वो जो जलते हैं मेरी ऊँचाइयों को देख कर,
मेरी दुआ है, खुदा बक़्श दे उनको भी एक पंखों का जोड़ा।

6.

My Stubborn Passion

This poem is based on all those negative people who cause problems for positive people with their negativity. Such people should not underestimate others. The poem is not based on any one individual in specific but it is a warning by the fearless pen to the negativity. With our passion & strong positivity, we can fight such negativity.

The ones, who are jealous to see my heights (growth),
I pray to The God, that he gives them also a pair of wings.

My personality is that, I take along even my enemies,
But at the times, I know very well how to walk alone.

It is the nature of time, that it changes,
But it is not my nature to change colours (attitudes) in changing times.

The ones who change their colours like chameleon,
I have learned to read people, from some Friends like such.

Don't underestimate me, just considering a flying particle
of dust,
I have the art to join the particles to create a flood (storm).

Leave your ambitions to imprison me,
This is my stubborn passion & not a pet horse.

The ones, who conspire hard to destroy me,
They don't know, how The God punishes (to such
negative people).

You feel happy, throwing me in the fire (tough situations),
I know how to become gold in firing blaze.

You never had a right to play with my sentiments,
My silence has a blaze, just attempt to touch sometime, if
you have the guts.

You may have a capacity to trim my wings,
My passions have the power to fly on it's own.

The ones who are jealous to see my heights,
I pray to The God, that he gives them also a pair of wings.

The Great Philanthropist & Businessman late Mr. Hayel Saeed Anam (HSA)

7

हयेल सईद अनाम – एक विचारधारा

यह कविता श्री हयेल सईद अनाम (HSA) के जीवन पर आधारित है। एक ऐसा जीवन, जिससे जितना सीखें, उतना कम है। उनका जन्म यमन देश के कराध गाँव में सन 1902 में हुआ। कई कठिन परिस्थितियों ओर जटिल चुनौतियों का सामना करते हुए उन्होंने एक विशाल औद्योगिक साम्राज्य बनाया, जिसे उनके नाम पर ऐच.ऐस.ए (HSA) के नाम से जाना जाता है। उन्होंने अपने जीवन काल में एक नेक दिल समाज सेवी के रूप में समाज के लिए बहुत काम किया। उन्होंने कई स्कूल एवं कॉलेज बनवा कर कई लोगों के सपने को साकार किया। 23 अप्रैल 1990 को जब उनका निधन हुआ, उन्होंने अपना एक हाथ ताबूत से बाहर रखने को कहा। ये उनका संदेश था, कि आप अपने साथ कुछ भी न ले जा पाएँगे और केवल आपके अच्छे कर्म आपके मरने के बाद भी आने वाली पीढ़ियों के दिलों में ज़िंदा रखेंगे। सही मायने में हयेल सईद अनाम (HSA) एक विचारधारा का नाम है।

कहते हैं बरसों लग जाते,
एक विचार पनपने को,
कितने ऋतु कितने मौसम बदलें,
एक मशाल के जलने को,
जाने कितनी सदियाँ लगतीं,
एक सोच बदलने को,
सोचो कितने युग लग जाते,
सरिता विचार की बहने को।

कई युगों में इक कोई विरला,
मशाल जलाने आता है,
अपने प्रकाश की आभा से,
जग को जग–मग कर जाता है,
जिसका जीवन मर कर भी,
दुनिया को राह दिखाता है,
और इक मिसाल बन जाता है,
वो "हयेल सईद अनाम HSA" कहलाता है।

कठिनाईयाँ जीवन में आईं,
फिर भी हार नहीं मानी,
जीवन में है आगे बढ़ना,
मन में थी बस ये ठानी,
पथरीले रास्तों पर शान से चलना,
सीखा था वो स्वाभिमानी,
कठिन परिश्रम, दृढ़ निश्चय,
उसके काम को दुनिया मानी।

मानवता के उस सेवक ने,
सबके दर्द को अपना माना,
औरों की ख़ातिर जीने को,
उसने खुदा की इबादत माना,
शिक्षा–ज्योति प्रज्ज्वलित कर उसने,
साकार किया हर जन का सपना,
हर क्षण–हर पल जीवन उसका,
सिखलाए कैसे जीवन जीना।

जब हुआ वो रुख़सत इस दुनिया से,
ख़ाली हाथ दिखा दुनिया को,
बोला कुछ न ले जाओगे,
ख़ाली हाथ मैं जाता हूँ
और ख़ाली हाथ तुम जाओगे,
जो जियोगे औरों की ख़ातिर,
मर के ज़िंदा रह जाओगे,
हयेल सईद अनाम – एक विचारधारा...

7.

Hayel Saeed Anam (HSA) - An Ideology

This Poem is based on the life of Mr. Hayel Saeed Anam (HSA). A man, you can learn as much as you can from his life and it will still be less. He was born in year 1902 in Qaradh village of Yemen. Facing bravely the tough circumstances & difficult challenges, he established a big business empire, that after his name, is known as HSA. As a Great philanthropist, he did great work for society. He built many schools & colleges and helped masses to fulfill their dreams. Just before he died on 23 April 1990, he told that his hand be kept out of his coffin. This was his message that as wealthy I may be, I am not taking anything with me and only the good deeds will keep one alive in the hearts of the coming generations. Truly, Hayel Saeed Anam (HSA) is the name of an Ideology.

It is believed, It takes years,
to get a thought cultivated,
Many-many seasons shuffle,
to get a torch enlightened (Revolutionary thoughts),
Don't know, how many centuries it takes,

to change the thinking,
Imagine, it takes many Eras,
for a river of Ideology to flow (to build an ideology).

In many eras, a rare special man,
Emerges from the masses to enlighten the torch
(Revolutionary Ideology),
And with the aura of his glow,
He enlightens the world,
His life, even after death,
shows the path of living to the world,
And the one who becomes a precedent (Role Model
context) for the world,
He is called "Hayel Saeed Anam" HSA.

He faced many hardships of life,
but never accepted defeat,
He progressed in life,
with Strong Determination,
The Self-esteemed Man learned,
to walk with The Splendour Elegance on the rocky paths
of life,
With Tough hard work & Strong determination,
his works in the world got recognition.

That Great Philanthropist,
considered others' griefs as his own grief,
He considered living for others,
as part of his worship to khuda (God),
Enlightening the refulgence of education,
He helped masses to make their dreams true,
Every minute & every moment his life teaches,
how one should lead life.

When he parted from this world,
He showed his bare hand to the world,
Symbolising the fact, that you can not take anything with
you to the grave,
I am going bare handed,
And you will also go empty handed,
But if you will live for others,
You will live even after death (Good deeds will be
remembered)
Hayel Saeed Anam (HSA) An Ideology...

8

इंडिया इंडोनेशिया

यह कविता भारत और इंडोनेशिया की गहरी मित्रता पर आधारित है। भारत और इंडोनेशिया की मित्रता 2019 में 70 वर्ष की हो गई है। इस स्वर्णिम पल को यादगार बनाने के लिए यह कविता मैंने लिखी है। कविता में दोनों महान राष्ट्रों में समानताओं को दर्शाया गया है। भारत और इंडोनेशिया की मित्रता और भी प्रफुल्लित हो, यही कामना है।

इंडिया इंडोनेशिया
चलेंगे साथ–साथ,
बढ़ेंगे साथ–साथ,
उन्नती के शिखरों पर,
चढ़ेंगे साथ–साथ।

इंडिया इंडोनेशिया
कितनी है समानता,
अनेकता में एकता,
एक एशिया का ताज,
एक पर्ल ऑफ़ एशिया,

इंडिया इंडोनेशिया
"मोदी"– "जोकोवी" दोनों हैं महारथी,
ऊँचे सपने – पक्के निश्चय,
और है मन में सादगी,
दुनिया कहे वाह! अटूट मित्रता।

इंडिया इंडोनेशिया
"रामायण" के अंश यहाँ,
"काकाविन रामायण" में मिलते हैं,
क्रिशन अर्जुन की "महाभारत" को,
इंडोनेशिया कहे "भारतयुद्धा"।

इंडिया इंडोनेशिया
"बाली" के कण—कण में,
"शिव" की आराधना,
कहते हैं "ऋषि मार्कण्डेय",
ने भी करी यहाँ साधना।

इंडिया इंडोनेशिया
सदियों से जोड़े हमें "हिंद महासागर",
सभ्यता को जोड़े "प्रमबनान मंदिर",
व्यापार हमें जोड़ता—संगीत हमें जोड़ता,
"ओड़ीशा" मनाए त्योहार "बालीजात्रा।"

इंडिया इंडोनेशिया
दोनो ही मनाते रामदान और ईद,
देते हैं दुनिया को शांति की सीख,
दिवाली, वैसाक और क्रिसमस मनाएँ,
क्या कहने इनकी धर्म—निरपेक्षता।

इंडिया इंडोनेशिया
"नेहरू"—"सुकर्नो" की दोस्ती कमाल,
"मोदी"—"जोकोवी" मित्रता बेमिसाल,
इंडिया इंडोनेशिया — हैं हाथों में हाथ,
ये मित्रता प्रफुल्लित हो लगें चार चाँद।

इंडिया इंडोनेशिया
चलेंगे साथ—साथ,
बढ़ेंगे साथ—साथ,
इंडिया इंडोनेशिया

8.

India Indonesia

Just as the name suggests, this poem Is based on the close friendship of the two countries India & Indonesia. This friendship turned 70 Years in 2019. I have written this poem to commemorate this golden moment. The similarities between the two great nations have been portrayed. I wish, that this friendship between India & Indonesia continue to flourish even more.

India Indonesia
will march together,
will progress together,
will climb up,
the peak of development together.

India Indonesia
There are so many similarities,
Unity in Diversity,
One is Crown of Asia,
And other Pearl of Asia.

India Indonesia
"Modi"-"Jokowi"are both Great Leaders,
High dreams Firm determination,

And they have simplicity in their hearts,
The world says Wow! Unbreakable Friendship.

India Indonesia
We find the elements of "Ramayana",
in "Kakawin Ramayana",
"Mahabharta" of Krishna Arjuna,
Indonesia calls it "Bharatayudha."

India Indonesia
"Shiva" is worshipped,
In every bit of "Bali",
It is believed that,
Maharishi Markandeya also did worship here.

India Indonesia
We are connected by Indian Ocean since ages,
Prambanan Temple connects our Civilizations,
Business connects us – Music connects us,
Odisha (a state of India) celebrates the festival "Bali Jatra"
(Voyage to Bali).

India Indonesia
Both celebrates Ramadan & Eid,
And give preaching of Peace to the World,
Both celebrate Diwali, Vaisak & Christmas,
Their secularism is worth admiring.

India Indonesia
"Nehru"-"Sukarno" friendship was wonderful,
"Modi"-"Jokowi" friendship is matchless,
India Indonesia walk hand in hand,
May this friendship flourish & achieve the Highest Glory.

India Indonesia
will march together,
will progress together,
India Indonesia

Mrs. Uttra Sharma & Prof. Harinder Sharma

9

काश ! मैं वक़्त को रोक पाता

यह कविता मैंने अपने आदरणीय माता–पिता श्रीमति उत्तरा शर्मा और प्रोफ. हरिंदर शर्मा जी को समर्पित की है। अपने माँ–बाप की कुर्बानियों की देन हम कभी नहीं दे पाते। काश! हम वक़्त को रोक पाते और हमेशा माँ–बाप का हाथ हमारे सर पर रहता। परमात्मा उन्हें लंबी आयु प्रदान करें, यही कामना है।

तो क्या हुआ, बड़े होने की ज़िद में कुछ कह नहीं पाता हूँ
पर आज भी, इस दिल को बचपन की तरह ही धड़कता हुआ पाता हूँ
आज भी बचपन की उसी मासूमियत से एक कंधा ढूँढा करता हूँ
आज भी ७ का पहाड़ा सुना कर, भाग के लिपट जाना चाहता हूँ।

वक़्त की सिलवटों को हटा कर जब भी देखा करता हूँ
हमेशा हर पल, आपको अपने पास खड़ा पाता हूँ
आपकी कुर्बानियाँ के आगे, एक अंश मात्र भी मेरी हस्ति नहीं,
ग़ज़ब है ख़ज़ाना आपकी दुआओं का, बरक़त जिसकी कभी घटती नहीं।

यादों की गलियों में, लमहों के झरोखों से, जब भी झाँका है,
वही बरसों पहले सा नूर आपका, चम–चमाता है,
वही नूर आज भी, अपनी रौशनाई से हमें रास्ता दिखाता है,
रहे सलामत आपका साया हम पे, ये दिल बस यही चाहता है।

चेहरे की इन झुर्रियों में कई बरसों का बसेरा है,
आज भी उँगली पकड़, खिलौने की ज़िद का मन मेरा है,
काश ! मैं वक़्त को रोक पाता, बेबस हूँ! मेरी चलती नहीं।
फिर मिले जीवन आप संग, ये हसरत कभी घटती नहीं।

तो क्या हुआ, बड़े होने की ज़िद में कुछ कह नहीं पाता हूँ...

9.

Wish I could hold Time

I have dedicated this poem to my respected parents Mrs. Uttra Sharma & Prof. Harinder Sharma. We can never repay the sacrifices of our parents, but just wish that we could hold time & always have our parents stay with us with their blessings. I wish, the kind God to give them a long life.

What if in stubbornness of being grown up, I am not able to say it,
even today, I find my heart beating like as in childhood,
even Today also, I try to find a shoulder, with all innocence of childhood,
even today also, I want to hug you, after reciting table of 7.

Whenever I iron kinks of the past time,
I have always found you standing by me,
My existence is not even a small bit, when compared with the sacrifices you have made for me,
The treasure of your blessings is wonderful, it's showering never fades.

Whenever I have peeped in, from the windows of moments, in the memory lanes,
Your ages old luster always shines brightly,
The same luster, even today, shows us the path with its glare,
This heart just wishes, Your shadow always stay with us.

There are many years wrapped in the wrinkles of your face,
Even today, holding your finger, I have a desire to insist for a toy,
Wish ! I could hold time, I am helpless ! It's not in my control,
We get a life with you again, this desire never reduces.

What if in stubbornness of being grown up, I am not able to say it...

10

कुछ बातें अपने आप से

यह कविता अपने आप से कुछ बातों पर आधारित है। जीवन में हर पल अपना विश्लेषण करना आवश्यक है, इसी से हमें सही मार्ग दर्शन मिलता है।

कुछ बातें अपने आप से,
कुछ बातें अपनी साख से,
कुछ बातें अपने वजूद से,
कुछ बातें वतने– सुरूर से,
कुछ बातें अपनी सोच से,
कुछ बातें अपनी रूह से,
कुछ बातें अपने जोश से,
कुछ बातें अपने होश से,
कुछ बातें ज़िद्दी जुनून से,
कुछ बातें उबलते खून से,
कुछ बातें असर हैं छोड़तीं,
कुछ बातें रुख़ को मोड़तीं,
कुछ बातें मन झंझोरतीं,
कुछ बातें दिलों को जोड़तीं,
कुछ बातें न हों तो बेहतर,
कुछ बातें हो जाएँ तो बेहतर,
कुछ बातें बात टटोलतीं,
कुछ बातें राज़ भी खोलतीं,
कुछ बातें कल को खोजतीं,

कुछ बातें आज का सोचतीं,
कुछ बातें गुज़रे वक़्त की,
कुछ बातें पत्थर सख़्त सीं,
कुछ बातें दिल का हैं मरहम,
कुछ बातें जैसे हों सरगम,
कुछ बातें मेरे अपनों की,
कुछ बातें उनके सपनों की,
कुछ बातें हैं कुर्बानियाँ,
कुछ बातें बेईमानियाँ,
कुछ बातें बहुत ज़रूरी हैं,
कुछ बातें बस मजबूरी हैं,
कुछ बातें बस बातें भर हैं,
कुछ बातें रेखा पत्थर की,
कुछ बातें देश–समाज की,
कुछ बातें इस संसार की,
कुछ बातें सब को जोड़तीं,
कुछ बातें रिश्ते तोड़तीं,
कुछ बातें राम रहीम की,
कुछ बातें होली ईद की,
कुछ बातें उस के नूर की,
कुछ बातें रब हुज़ूर की,
कुछ बातें करिए सोच के,
कुछ बातें बोलें तोल के,
कुछ बातें बात संभालतीं,
कुछ बातें बात बिगाड़तीं,
कुछ बातें अड़ियल ज़मीर से,
कुछ बातें मन गंभीर से,
कुछ बातें दिल की आस से,
कुछ बातें अपने आप से...

IO.

Some Talks with the Self

This poem is based on some talks with my own self. It is important in life that every moment we do a self-introspection, it gives us a right path to follow in the life.

Some talks with the self,
Some talks with my credence,
Some talks with my existence,
Some talks with my intoxication for the country,
Some talks with my thoughts,
Some talks with my soul,
Some talks with my enthusiasm,
Some talks with my consciousness,
Some talks with my steadfast passion,
Some talks with boiling blood,
Some talks leave impressions,
Some talks turn the paths,
Some talks shake the mind,
Some talks bind hearts,
Some talks, better not said,
Some talks are better if said,
Some talks try to find hidden meanings,
Some talks open secrets,
Some talks searching tomorrow,

Some talks thinking today,
Some talks of the past,
Some talks are hard as stone,
Some talks are healing for the heart,
Some talks are melody,
Some talks are of my own (relationships),
Some talks of their dreams,
Some talks are sacrificial,
Some talks are dishonest,
Some talks are very important,
Some talks are just compulsion,
Some talks are just talks,
Some talks are line on stone (permanent),
Some talks of nation & society,
Some talks of this world,
Some talks bind everyone,
Some talks break relations,
Some talks of Ram & Rahim,
Some talks of Holi & Eid,
Some talks of its luster (The God's luster),
Some talks of The Kind God,
Some talks, say after thinking carefully,
Some talks, say after evaluating meaningfully,
Some talks save the moments,
Some talks spoil the moments,
Some talks with my stubborn conscious,
Some talks with my solemn mind,
Some talks with desire of heart,
Some talks with the self...

11

ख़ामोश परिंदे

यह कविता जीवन की उस कड़वी सच्चाई पर आधारित है, जहाँ मौकापरस्त लोग अपने फ़ायदे के लिए दूसरों का इस्तेमाल और शोषण करते हैं। ऐसे लोगों को समझना चाहिए कि बुराई की उम्र कभी भी लंबी नहीं हुआ करती।

दिलों में चोर हो, तो नज़रें मिला नहीं करतीं,
ज़मीर पे बोझ हो, तो नज़रें उठा नहीं करती,
नज़र की बात है,नज़रियों का बदल जाना,
नंज़र से गिर कर,फिर क़दर हुआ नहीं करती।

कंधे हाज़िर हैं मेरे, सीढ़ियाँ बनाने को,
छुओ तुम आसमां, न उफ़ करेंगे हम ज़माने को,
आसमां तुम्हारा सही ! पर ज़मीं तो न छीनो हमसे,
ऐ नादां ! बिना ज़मीं के भी जन्नत मिला नहीं करती।

लहू सफ़ेद हो जाए, तो सुर्ख़ रंग कहाँ ढूँढें,
ज़मीर जो सिक्कों में तुल जाए,तो ईमान कहाँ ढूँढें,
झूठ के बाज़ार में, जो बेईमान बेच रहा सच्चाई को,
पूछो उसको कि सच और ईमान कहाँ ढूँढें।

वो बात, जो खून—ए—जिगर कर दे मेरा,
ताज्जुब है ! सितमगर पे असर नहीं करती,
देखे हैं हमने, ख़ामोश परिंदों की आह से टूटते तरकश,
उम्मीद वो समझें ! कुफ़्र की उम्र लंबी हुआ नहीं करती।

II.

Silent Birds

This poem is based on such bitter truth of the life, where the opportunists use & exploit others for their benefits. Such people should understand that evil doesn't have a long life.

If hearts have wrong intentions, one can't see eye to eye,
If conscious has a burden (of wrong deeds), one can't live with dignity,
One changes its viewpoint with observations,
Once you lose respect in someone perception, it's difficult to get respect.

I offer my shoulders to make ladders for you to climb (in the context of people who just use others to grow),
You touch the Sky, I won't express my pain to the world,
Let the Sky be yours, but don't snatch my space on land,
O Fool ! Without land you can't get heavens.

If the blood turns white, from where to find the Red colour (in context of compromising values of life),
If the conscience is sold, from where to find honesty,
In the market of lies, the dishonest who is selling the truth,
Ask him, from where to find the truth & integrity.

Something that hurts me deep,
Surprisingly! that doesn't affect the evil (the one who tortures context),
I have seen, the quivers breaking with the groan of silent (poor) birds,
Hope he understands! The evil doesn't have a long life.

12

यादों की एक पोटली

यह कविता जीवन की ऐसी सुखद यादों पर आधारित है, जिन्हें हम भुला कर भी नहीं भुला पाते। ये यादें मानो एक पोटली में बंद हैं और यदि यह पोटली खुल जाए तो बड़े प्रयत्न से भी बंद करनी मुश्किल हो जाती है।

यादों की एक पोटली,
जाने किसने खोल दी,
करता हूँ ये जतन समेटूँ
न बँधती जो खोल दी।

बचपन के वो खेल–खिलौने,
सोना ज़िद में नानी सिरहाने,
वक़्त ने ऐसी करवट बदली,
अब मैंने ज़िद छोड़ दी।

मैं तो क़समों पे मरता था,
वायदों का क़ायदा पढ़ता था,
फिर कुछ ऐसे धोखे खाए,
क़सम वो मैंने तोड़ दी।

बचपन बीता गया लड़कपन,
पलक झपकते गुज़रा यौवन,
रेत वक़्त का फिसला जाए,
अब गिनती मैंने छोड़ दी।

याद बहुत आते हैं वो दिन,
लड़ना आपस में तारे गिन,
चाहता था रखूँ सब दिल में,
क्यूँ कैसे कब बोल दी।

भाई संग नटखट अठखेली,
करें शरारत बन मन–मौजी,
जीवन–चक्र का पाठ पढ़ा तो,
शराफ़त मैंने ओढ़ ली।

ये यादों की पोटली ऐसी,
जितना खोलो खुलती जाती,
लम्हों के अनगिनत समंदर,
जाने कैसे सोखती।

यादों की एक पोटली...

12.

A Bundle of Memories

This poem is based on such pleasant memories of life, which we cannot forget at all. These memories are such, as if packed in a bundle & once the bundle is opened, it's very difficult to repack.

A Bundle of memories,
I don't know, who opened it,
I am trying my best,
but not able to tie it again, once opened.

The games & toys of my childhood,
I always persisted to stay with my grandmother (Nani),
The time changed its side in such a way,
I have left my stubbornness behind.

I would die for my promises,
I used to follow the promises as law,
I was then betrayed in many ways,
I broke my own rules to follow promises.

The childhood passed by,
The adolescence passed by with flick of an eye,
The sand of time is slipping,
I am left counting (Years).

I miss those days a lot,
when we (siblings) used to fight counting stars,
I wanted to keep all in my heart,
I don't why, how & when I spoke all this.

Those naughty childhood games with brother,
when we were making mischiefs, being care free,
when I read the lesson of life cycle,
I have embraced decency.

This bundle of memories is such,
more you open, it keeps opening (revealing),
strange how it absorbs,
the countless oceans of moments.

A Bundle of memories...

13.

बस बहुत हुआ !!!!

यह कविता भारत में हुए पुलवामा आतंकी हमले और उस जैसे सभी आतंकी हमलों में आक्रोश स्वरूप में लिखी गई है। अगर शत्रु प्यार और सौहार्द की भाषा न समझे तो समय आ गया है कि उसे उसी की भाषा में मुँहतोड़ जवाब दे कर समझाया जाए। जय हिंद... वंदे मातरम।

बस बहुत हुआ,
बाँध सबर का टूट के चकनाचूर हुआ,
अब आर या पार ही हो जाए,
बस प्यार–व्यार अब बहुत हुआ।

जब दुश्मन प्यार नहीं समझे,
नफ़रत की भाषा ही बोले,
हम फूलों की बारिश करते,
वो आग के गोले ही दागे।

ना समझें वो हमको कायर,
हम चुप हैं अमन की ही ख़ातिर,
पर जो हमको ललकारोगे,
हम बरसेंगे बन कर शोले।

चीतों–शेरों की बस्ती में,
जब गीदड़ आने लग जाएँ,
न बाँधो फिर तुम शेरों को,
गीदड़ को घर में घुस मारें।

सावधान ! अब बहुत हुआ,
खबरदार ! अब बहुत हुआ,
ग़ैरत से मेरी मत खेलो,
धैर्य को मेरे मत परखो,

बस बहुत हुआ !!!!

13.

It's Enough ...

It's enough,
The barrage of patience has broken apart,
Let there be a solution for once,
It's enough of love & talks.

When the enemy doesn't understand the love,
and it always speaks the language of hatred,
We shower flowers,
and it drops bombs of fire on us.

They dare not consider us cowards,
We are silent, just for the sake of peace,
But, if some one will challenge us,
We will shower like fire blaze.

When the jackals (Terrorists) start entering,
in the colony of leopards & lions (Brave Indians),
then don't tie the lions,
and make them free to kill the jackals in their house.

Caution ! It's Enough,
Warning ! It's Enough,
Don't dare to play with my dignity,
Don't dare to test my patience

It's Enough !!!!

14.

Life माने ज़िंदगी बस यूँ ही !

यह कविता एक हल्की–फुल्की कविता है, जो सरल तरीक़े से जीवन के सभी पहलुओं का चित्रण करती है। जीवन में सुख और दुख दोनों ही रहते हैं। कविता अंत में यह संदेश देती है कि हमें जीवन को हर हाल में स्वीकार कर इसके संग खुल कर जीना चाहिए।

कटते–कटते कट जाती है,
हँसते–रोते गुज़र जाती है,
कभी ये Naughty गुदगुदाती है,
कभी Seriously Serious हो जाती है।
Life माने ज़िंदगी बस यूँ ही !

मीठी रबड़ी सी कभी लगती,
कभी खट्टी इमली बन जाती है,
थोड़ी नमकीन थोड़ी मिर्ची,
करेले से कड़वी भी बन जाती है,
Life माने ज़िंदगी बस यूँ ही !

बरगद की छाया कभी देती,
कभी Cactus सी चुभ जाती है,
कभी खुशबू गुलाब–गुलदस्ता सी,
बे–रंग कभी ये बन जाती है,
Life माने ज़िंदगी बस यूँ ही !

कभी खुशी के झोंके लाती,
कभी ग़मों के दिन दिखलाती,
चाँद की शीतलता भी इसमें,
कभी तपती रेत सी बन जाती,
Life माने ज़िंदगी बस यूँ ही !

कभी इसकी करती बात,
कभी उसकी जोहती बाट,
कभी मधुर मिलन की दे सौग़ात,
कभी दर्द–जुदाई दे जाती है,
Life माने ज़िंदगी बस यूँ ही !

ये आए जैसे, आने दो,
हर रंग जियो, हर ढंग जियो,
ये Life मिली है एक बार,
हर हाल में इसके संग जियो,
Life माने ज़िंदगी बस यूँ ही !

14.

Life means ZINDAGI Just like that!

This poem is a light poem, which portrays every aspect of life in a simple way. Life has both happiness & sorrows. In the end, the poem gives the message that we should live our life fully & accept it as it comes.

It just passes by,
It passes by laughing & crying,
Some times it tickles being naughty,
Some times it becomes very serious,
Life means ZINDAGI Just like that!

Some times it is sweet as a dessert (Rabri is an Indian Desert),
Some times it becomes sour like tamarind,
A Little salty little chilly,
Some times it becomes bitter than bitter gourd,
Life means ZINDAGI Just like that!

Sometimes it gives shade as a banyan tree,
Sometimes it pricks as a cactus,
Sometimes it has fragrance of a rose bouquet,
Sometimes it becomes colourless,
Life means ZINDAGI Just like that!

Sometimes it brings a spurt of happiness,
Sometimes it shows days of sorrow,
It has calmness as the moon,
Sometimes it becomes hot sand (like desert),
Life means ZINDAGI Just like that!

Sometimes it talks about someone (General context),
Sometimes it waits for someone,
Sometimes it presents sweet rendezvous,
Sometimes it gives pain of severance,
Life means ZINDAGI Just like that!

Let it come, the way it comes,
Live every colour & every bit of it,
We have got this life for once,
Live with it in every condition,

15.

सिस्टम का जनाज़ा

यह कविता कुछ वर्ष पहले भारत के एक प्रांत में हुई एक घटना पर आधारित है, जब एक ग़रीब आदमी अपनी पत्नी की लाश को अपने कंधे पर रख कर कई किलोमीटर चला। प्रशासन उसे एक एंबुलेंस भी न दे पाया। यह कविता किसी सरकार, प्रशासन, व्यक्तिविशेष, राजनैतिक दल एवं संगठन के विरुद्ध नहीं है बल्कि हमारे सोए सिस्टम को जगाने का एक प्रयास है।

आज सुबह जब उठा तो टीवी पर एक ख़बर थी,
सुबह की सुस्त आँखों को मला तो,
धुँधली तस्वीर साफ़ दिखने लगी,
एक पतला सा आदमी अपने कंधे पर,
एक लंबी सी गठड़ी लिए जा रहा था,
पीछे–पीछे एक छोटी लड़की चल रही थी,
टी.वी. की आवाज़ को ऊँचा किया तो,
यक़ीन मानिए कमरे में तो आवाज़ हो गई,
पर दिल–ओ–दिमाग़ में अजीब सा सन्नाटा छा गया,
ये गठड़ी उस ग़रीब की बीवी की लाश थी,
छोटी लड़की अपनी माँ की एक कंधे की अर्थी के पीछे आँसू
बहाती चल रही थी,
हमारा लाचार सिस्टम, हमारा बीमार प्रशासन इस ग़रीब को एक
एंबुलैंस भी न दे पाया,
शायद, बीमार सिस्टम ने एंबुलैंस अपने लिए रखी होगी,
क्या पता कब इसे भी ज़रूरत पड़ जाए!!!!

विडंबना ....
ये एक ग़रीब की शव यात्रा नहीं थी ....
ये हमारे लाचार सिस्टम का जनाज़ा था ....
ये हमारे बीमार प्रशासन की शव यात्रा थी ....
ये हमारी मुर्दा संवेदनशीलता की एक काली सच्चाई थी ....
अफ़सोस ....
हम १२५ करोड़ भारतीय इस शव यात्रा में चुप–चाप ख़ामोशी से
शामिल थे।

15.

The System's Pyre …

This poem is based on an incident that occurred a few years ago, in one of the states of India, where a poor man walked many kilometres, with the dead body of his wife on his shoulders. The administration could not provide him even with an ambulance. This poem is not against any one government, administration, person in specific, political party or organisation, but it is an effort to wake up our sleeping system.

When I woke up this morning, there was a news on TV,
when I rubbed my lazy morning eyes,
I started seeing the blurred image, clear,
one thin man, on his shoulder,
was carrying a long bundle,
a small girl was following him,
when I raised the volume of the TV,
trust me! there was sound in the room,
but the mind & heart became totally silent & blank,
this bundle was the dead body of wife of this poor man,
the small girl, was following with tearing eyes, the one
shouldered pyre of her mother,
our paralysed system, our sick administration could not
provide even an ambulance to this poor man,

may be! the sick system kept the ambulance for itself,
who knows when would it need it,
Sad...
This was not the funeral of a poor lady,
This was the funeral of our paralysed system,
This was the funeral of our sick administration,
This was the black truth of our dead sensitivity,
Regret...
We, 125 crores Indians silently joined them in this funeral.

Ashish presenting a copy of the poem to The Former Consul General of India in Medan, Dr. Shalia Shah

16.

नमस्ते मीडान इंडियन बाज़ार

यह कविता मीडान, इंडोनेशिया में भारत के प्रधान कोंसलावास द्वारा आयोजित एक भारतीय बाज़ार पर आधारित है। मीडान में रहते हुए मुझे और मेरे परिवार को बहुत करीब से भारत के प्रधान कोंसलावास के साथ काम करने का अवसर मिला। इंडियन ऐक्सपेट्रीयेट्स एसोसिएशन मीडान (IEAM) के अध्यक्ष होने के नाते मुझे भारतीय समुदाय की सेवा का अवसर प्राप्त हुआ, यह मेरा सौभाग्य है। यह कविता मैंने "नमस्ते मीडान बाज़ार" के उपलक्ष्य में लिख कर मीडान, इंडोनेशिया में भारत के प्रधान कोंसलावास को समर्पित की। इस कविता की एक प्रति मैंने उस समय के मीडान में भारत के आदरणीय कौंसल जनरल डा. शालिया शाह जी को "नमस्ते मीडान बाज़ार" में भेंट की।

रंग—बिरंगे कपड़े पहनो, हो जाओ तैयार,
मीडान क्लब में होने वाली मस्ती की बौछार,
20 नवंबर भूल ना जाना, दिन छुट्टी इतवार,
इंडियन कंसुलेट ले के आया "नमस्ते मीडान इंडियन बाज़ार"

भारतीय व्यंजन खूब मिलेंगे, आलू पूरी संग अचार,
इडली मुँह में पानी लाए, कचौरी की भरमार,
बिरयानी के बाद सही में एक लड्डू बनता है यार,
इंडियन कंसुलेट ले के आया "नमस्ते मीडान इंडियन बाज़ार"

बच्चों संग बच्चे बन जाओ, खेलो गेम्स बार–अं–बार,
घुमा के रिंग टेबल पे मारो, कुछ तो आ जाएगा हाथ,
ना ना बिलकुल ना शर्माओ, जीतो ईनाम हर इक बार,
इंडियन कंसुलेट ले के आया "नमस्ते मीडान इंडियन बाज़ार"

रंग–बिरंगी फुलकारी ने रंग बिखेरे कई हज़ार,
नैकलेस, पर्स और बहुत कुछ, भरा हुआ है सब बाज़ार,
मेहंदी देखो खूब सजेगी, आ जाएगी तीज की याद,
इंडियन कंसुलेट ले के आया "नमस्ते मीडान इंडियन बाज़ार"

बिज़नेस की बातें भी होंगी, बुक करवाओ ट्रक ओर कार,
योग गुरु की बातों को सुन कर बनाओ योग जीवन–आधार,
20 नवंबर भूल ना जाना, दिन छुट्टी इतवार,
इंडियन कंसुलेट ले के आया "नमस्ते मीडान इंडियन बाज़ार"

16.

Namaste Medan Indian Bazar

This poem is based on "Namaste Medan Bazaar" event organized by The Consulate General of India in Medan, Indonesia. During our stay in Medan, my family and I got an opportunity to work closely with The Consulate General of India in Medan. I feel blessed, that as President Convener of Indian Expatriates Association Medan (IEAM), I got an opportunity to serve the Indian community. I wrote this poem to commemorate this bazaar, and I dedicate the poem to The Consulate General of India in Medan. I presented a copy of this poem to the then Hon'ble Consul General of India in Medan Dr. Shalia Shah, during "Namaste Medan bazaar".

Wear colourful clothes, and get ready,
There is going to be a shower of fun in Medan Club,
Don't forget, it's on Sunday 20 November,
Indian consulate brings "Namste Medan Indian Bazar".

There will be plenty of Indian cuisines, There will be Alu Puri with Pickle (Alu Puri is popular traditional Indian Cuisine), There will be mouth watering Idli & Lots of Kachori (Idli & Kachori are traditional Indian Cuisines),

After Biryani, My friend trust me! one Laddu is a must
(Biryani is traditional indian Rice & Laddu is Traditional
Indian sweet),
Indian consulate brings "Namste Medan Indian Bazar".

Be kids with kids & play lots of games,
Throw the lucky ring on table, hope you will win
something,
No no don't be shy at all, win the prizes repeatedly,
Indian consulate brings "Namste Medan Indian Bazar".

The colourful Fulkari has spreaded thousands of colours
(Fulkari is a traditional hand embrioded Indian cloth for
ladies),
There is Necklace, Purses & so many things, all Bazar is full,
The henna will adore the hands & You will remember Teej
(Teej is a Indian women's festival),
Indian consulate brings "Namste Medan Indian Bazar".

There will be business discussions also, You can book a
truck & car,
Listening to teachings of Yoga trainer, Make Yoga as way
of life,
Don't forget, it's on Sunday 20 November,
Indian consulate brings "Namste Medan Indian Bazar".

17.

दिल का टुकड़ा

यह कविता मैंने तब लिखी, जब मेरी बेटी अपूर्वा, अपने जीवन का एक नया अध्याय लिखने के लिए, उच्च शिक्षा हेतु मेलबर्न, आस्ट्रेलिया जा रही थी। सच में यह क्षण, माता–पिता के लिए एक गर्व का तो होता है पर यही लगता है मानो आपके दिल का टुकड़ा दिल से अलग हो कर जा रहा हो।

दिल का टुकड़ा,
दिल से हो कर दूर चला है,
फिर भी दिल पूछे है खुद से,
ओ पगले, दिल क्यूँ रोता है।

दिल, दिल में ही सोच रहा है,
गुम–सुम गुप–चुप ताक रहा है,
दिल का टुकड़ा पलक झपकते,
समय लाँघ कर बड़ा हुआ है।

आएँगी पथ में बाधाएँ,
पथरीली होंगी कुछ राहें,
हिम्मत से आगे तू बढ़ना,
इस दिल की है यही तमन्ना।

जा तू हर सपने के पा ले,
अपनी मेहनत, दृढ़ निश्चय से,
हर मुश्किल आसान बना ले,
इस दिल की बस यही दुआ है।

दिल का टुकड़ा,
दिल से हो के दूर चला है...

17.

Piece of My Heart

I wrote this poem, when my daughter Apurva was going away, to write a new chapter of her life in Melbourne, Australia, for her higher studies. Truly, this moment is always a moment of pride for all parents but it also looks as if a piece of your heart is going away from you.

Piece of my heart,
Is parting away from my heart,
surprisingly ! still the heart is asking itself,
O ! insane heart why are you crying.

The heart is thinking,
Silently it is watching,
The piece of heart has grown up jumping ahead of times,
with the flick of an eye.

There will be obstacles on the way,
There will be stony paths,
You march ahead with courage,
This heart has only this desire.

May you fulfil all your dreams,
With your hardwork & firm determination,
May you solve all problems,
This heart has just this orison.

Piece of my heart,
Is parting away from heart.

18.

आज़ादी और नव–चेतना

यह कविता हमें अपनी आज़ादी की अहमियत बताती है। हमें ये स्वतंत्रता शहीदों की कुर्बानियों के बाद प्राप्त हुई है। कविता यह प्रेरित करती है कि हमें ऐसी नव–चेतना जगानी है कि हम अपने प्राणों की आहुति दे कर भी अपने भारत और इसकी स्वतंत्रता की रक्षा करेंगे।

आज़ादी तेरी आन का सदक़ा,
मातृभूमि के मान का सदक़ा,
भारत माँ की जय का नारा,
शंखनाद से हो जयकारा,
जन–जन जागे,
कण–कण जागे,
रोम–रोम में ज्वाला जागे,
बच्चा–बच्चा दे हुंकारा,
लाओ कहीं से वो चेतना,
नव–साधना, नव–प्रेरणा।

आज़ादी की राहों में,
कोई आँच न आने देंगे हम,
मर जाएंगे मिट जाएँगे,
राष्ट्र न मिटने देंगे हम,
आज़ादी की ख़ातिर,
अपने प्राणों की कुरबानी दें,

देश की ख़ातिर जन्मे हैं,
और देश पे जान लुटा भी दें,
लाओ कहीं से वो चेतना,
नव—साधना, नव—प्रेरणा।

आज समय है एक हो जाएँ,
जात भूल कर, प्रांत भूल कर,
एक भारत का बिगुल बजाएँ,
आज समय है कुछ कर जाएँ,
वीरों की अमर शहादत का,
अपने लहू से क़र्ज़ चुकाएँ,
मिली आज़ादी बलिदानों से,
आओ मिल कर शीश निवाएँ,
लाओ कहीं से वो चेतना,
नव—साधना, नव—प्रेरणा।

18.

Freedom & The New Sentience

This poem reminds us of the importance of our freedom. We have received this freedom after the sacrifices of our martyrs. The poem inspires us to create such a new sentience, so that we can protect our India & its freedom, even if it means by sacrificing our lives.

For the dignity of the Freedom,
For the honour of the Motherland,
With the victory slogan of Mother India,
Let it be a holy roar,
Let the masses be enlightened,
Let each bit & corner (of India) be enlightened,
Let it be blaze inside (Revolutionary awakening),
Let every child roar,
Let's bring such a sentience,
The new accomplishment, the new inspiration.

We will not allow,
any compromise with freedom,
We will die,
But will not allow the country to die,
We will sacrifice our lives,
for sake of freedom,

We have taken birth for country,
and will sacrifice our lives for the country,
Let's bring such a sentience,
The new accomplishment, the new inspiration.

Today the time demands, that we be one,
Forgetting the castes, forgetting the states,
We play the bugle of one India,
Today the time demands, that we do something (special),
With our blood, we will repay,
The immortal sacrifice of our brave soldiers (Freedom Fighters),
We have got this freedom from sacrifices,
Let's all bow our heads (for it's respect & dignity),
Let's bring such a sentience,
The new accomplishment, the new inspiration.

19.

अपनी मिट्टी की खुशबू

यह कविता उन सभी प्रवासी भारतियों की भावनाओं को व्यक्त करती है, जो जब अपने देश भारत आने के लिए जहाज़ में बैठते हैं और तभी से उनको अपने वतन की मिट्टी की भीनी खुशबू आने लग जाती है। मेरा यही संदेश है – "दुनिया को अपनी सकारात्मक सोच की बाँहों से गले लगा लो, तो दुनिया आपको अपने दयालु भाव से आपको अपना लेगी।"

अपनी मिट्टी की वो खुशबू,
सौंधी–सौंधी सी आने लगी,
अपनी गलियों की वो रौनक़,
फिर अपनी झलक दिखाने लगी,
अपने बाग़ों की वो चिड़ियाँ,
कुछ गीत नए से गाने लगीं,
अपने लोगों की वो बातें,
मरहम सा दिल पे लगाने लगीं,
अपने बचपन की वो यादें,
इन आँखों में लहराने लगीं,
अपने यारों की वो महफ़िल,
फिर इस दिल को धड़काने लगीं,
अपने घर की भीनी सी महक़,
इस तन–मन को महकाने लगी,
मैं सोच रहा, क्या और कहूँ
क्या और अभी मैं बात करूँ,
शायद अब सब हैं बूझ गए,
किस डगर ये मेरी उड़ान चली :–)

19.

The Fragrance of my soil

This poem expresses the feelings of all NRIs, expatriates, who when board the plane to come back home to their country, India, they start to feel the fragrance of their homeground emanating. My message to all - "Embrace the world with Arms of Positivity and the world will embrace you in return with all its kindness".

I can feel,
the fragrance of my soil
I can feel,
the glimpse of Shine in my streets,
The sparrows of my garden,
have started singing new songs,
The soothing talks of my nears and dears,
are smearing on my heart,
The memories of my childhood,
have started rippling in my eyes,
The gathering of my friends,
Have set my heart beating again,
The pleasant fragrance of home,
Is blooming in my heart and soul,

I am thinking what to say more,
What more I should tell,
Perhaps! everyone has guessed by now
Where my flight is heading to :-)

20.

हीरे, पन्ने और मोती

यह कविता, मेरी तीनों पुस्तकों – "कुछ मोती दिल के सागर से", "कुछ हीरे मन की ख़ान से" और "कुछ पन्ने विचारों से तराशे हुए" का सारांश है। हमारे रिश्ते–नाते, सपने, आकांक्षाएँ, विचार, लक्ष्य, उद्देश्य, संस्कार, हमारे जीवन के बीते अच्छे–बुरे, सुखद–दुखद पल ये सभी जैसे हीरे, पन्ने और मोती जैसे अनमोल रत्न हैं। जीवन और कुछ नहीं बस इन्हीं का एक विशाल संग्रह है। पढ़ते रहिए, बढ़ते रहिए, खुश रहिए!

यादों से छीन के लाया मैं,
कुछ जीवन के अनमोल रत्न,
हीरे, पन्ने और मोती से,
कुछ बातें, लम्हे और वो दिन।

कुछ ग़ैर से हैं और कुछ अपने,
है शुक्र मिलाए उस रब ने,
हीरे, पन्ने और मोती से,
ये रिश्ते सागर से गहरे।

सपना है, छू लूँ आसमान,
है सोच में पंखों सी ताक़त
हीरे, पन्ने और मोती से,
ये जज़्बा, हिम्मत और मेहनत।

सच्ची बात पे अडिग रहूँ,
ईमान और कर्म मेरा परिचय,
हीरे, पन्ने और मोती से,
उसूल, ज़मीर और दृढ़ निश्चय।

ईश्वर का सुंदर निर्माण,
रखेंगे स्वच्छ ये है सौगंध,
हीरे, पन्ने और मोती से,
ये धरती, सागर और अम्बर।

जीवन के कुछ अनुभव ले कर,
सपने– लम्हे माला में पिरो कर,
लाया हूँ आपकी ख़िदमत में,
ये हीरे, पन्ने और मोती....

20.

Diamonds, Emeralds & Pearls

This poem is a conclusion of my three books - "PEARLS from the ocean of heart", "DIAMONDS from the mine of mind" & "EMERALDS carved with thoughts". Our relationships, dreams, ambitions, thoughts, goals, purposes, values, the good & bad, happy & sorrowful moments of life, all are precious gems like DIAMONDS, EMERALDS & PEARLS. Life is nothing but a big collection of all these. KEEP READING, KEEP MOVING, STAY HAPPY!

I have brought, snatching from Memories,
Some precious gems of life,
Like Diamonds, Emeralds & Pearls,
Some talks, moments & some days of life.

Some strangers & some own relations,
Thank God, he made us meet,
Like Diamonds, Emeralds & Pearls,
These relationships deeper than sea.

My dream is to touch the sky,
Power of wings in my thoughts,
Like Diamonds, Emeralds & Pearls,
My Passion, Courage & Hardwork.

I am steadfast on the truth,
Integrity & karma is my introduction,
Like Diamonds, Emeralds & Pearls,
My Principles, Conscious & Firm Determination.

The wonderful creation of The God,
We promise we will keep clean (Pollution Free),
Like Diamonds, Emeralds & Pearls,
This Earth, Oceans & Sky.

Taking some experiences of life,
Threading some dreams & moments in gorget,
I have brought for You (Readers),
These Diamonds, Emeralds & Pearls (My Poems) ....

Some Memories of Ashish's last two Publications

"PEARLS from the Ocean of Heart" - **"कुछ मोती दिल के सागर से"**

"DIAMONDS from the Mine of Mind" - **"कुछ हीरे मन की खान से"**

First copy being presented to The Almighty Shree Markandey Rishi Ji

First Book & Second book were released by Mrs.Savita Bhatti at Capital Book Depot in Chandigarh on 5th July 2014 & 27 June 2015 respectively. In left picture can be seen from left to right Prof.Harinder Sharma - Father of Ashish, Author - Ashish Sharma, Mrs.Savita Bhatti, Yogita Sharma – wife of Ashish and translator of book and Malini Nair – Head Publishing, Wordit CDE. In the right picture can be seen from left to right Late Sh.Kesar Dass Gambhir – Former President Shree Markandeshwar Mandir Sabha, Author – Ashish Sharma, Yogita Sharma – wife of Ashish and translator of book, Mrs.Savita Bhatti, Malini Nair – Head Publishing, Wordit CDE & Prof.Harinder Sharma - Father of Ashish

Madam Mrs. Savita Bhatti ji
addressing the gathering
at book release

Dr. Harjit Singh, a noted punjabi
poet giving his valuable inputs
at book release

Ashish interacting with media
& reciting his poems
at book release

Ashish's daughter Apurva (Aru)
reciting his poems
at book release

Media Reviews

The Tribune

Ashish Sharma's new book Kuch Heere Mann Ki Khan Se deals with emotional and social issues

HARLEEN KAUR

After the success of his first book, *Pearls from The Ocean of Heart* Ashish Sharma is back with his second poetry book— *Diamonds from The Mine of Mind/ Kuch Heere Mann Ki Khan Se*. The book was launched on Saturday. It has 20 poems, written in Hindi along with their translations in English, to overcome the language barrier. Ashish's wife, Yogita, helped him in the translation part.

The poet has expressed his thoughts about social evils and issues, environment, relationships, happiness and hope, in verses. Sensitive topics like terrorism, women empowerment, Partition and drug addiction also find mention in his book. The book also has a motivational poem for women, taking an inspiration from the Nirbhaya incident. An engineer and an MBA, Ashish is currently working as the general manager in a multinational company in Medan, Indonesia. He started writing poetry in his college days, taking an inspiration from ghazal maestro Jagjit Singh and rendering of his father's (Harivansh Rai Bachchan) poems by Amitabh Bachchan.

The poem titled *Ik ma ke the do pyare bete*/A mother had two sons is based on Partition. Then there is *Aaj ek ma ko mil ke lauta hu*/I met a mother today which deals with drug addiction. Another one titled *Nirbheek 'Nirbhaya' nirbhay ban*/Brave 'Nirbahaya' Be courageous, is a motivational poem for women. *Samay ki ret*/The sand of time is based on life. Another poem *Chlo aaj ik pedh lgayen*/Let's plant a tree deals with environmental issues. *Diamonds from The Mine of Mind* is priced at Rs 250.

WHITE TRACK: Ashish Sharma

Dainik Bhaskar

Rhymes and Reason

POETRY began with my love for music. I wanted to be a singer, but ended up being an electrical engineering. The melody in my head and heart never died, and what I had been writing for years has finally taken shape as my first collection of poems," says Ashish Sharma, who released his works in a book, *Kuch Moti Dil Ke Saagar Mein*, at Capitol Book Depot. The poems are in Hindi, with English translations alongside, and Sharma credits wife Yogita for helping him with it. Inspired by daily events, his personal journey, relationships and social issues, Sharma's poems express hope and optimism.

'I like to vent my ideas, anger and thoughts through poetry'

JAGMEETA THIND JOY
CHANDIGARH, JULY 6

THE MIND is always churning out thoughts and ideas and it's not often that one decides to put those thoughts on paper. But for Ashish Sharma, a general manager working with a multinational company in Medan in Indonesia, it was a "passion for poetry" that got him to write his second book, *Diamonds from the Mine of Mind/Kuch Heere Mann Ki Khan Se*, published by Open Crayons (Rs 250). He has previously written *Pearls from The Ocean of the Heart*, which was launched last year and well received. "There are many issues that I wanted to address this time like women empowerment, drug addiction, environment and Partition. I have done that through these poems," says Sharma who launched the book in the city recently.

The ambitiously titled book is a collection of 20 Hindi poems by Sharma with English translations by his wife, Yogita Sharma. "We didn't want language to be a barrier and therefore, decided to offer the translations as well," explains the author. The poems are inspired by day-to-day events and

ASHISH SHARMA

occurrences in the world and the poet's life. "In my life, I have been hugely inspired by the late humourist Jaspal Bhatti and I chose to write satire because of him," says Sharma who likes to pen his thoughts on current affairs. In his latest book, there's a poem titled *Nirbheek Nirbhaya Nirbhay Ban* (Brave Nirbahaya) dedicated to the girl child that draws from the Nirbhaya incident. "All of us feel strongly about the things that take place

The cover of the book *Diamonds from the Mine of Mind*. Express

around us. I like to vent my ideas, anger and thoughts through poetry," says the author. Although he took to poetry and polished his Urdu— he credits late ghazal singer Jagjit Singh for the same — in his college days, it's only recently that he decided to go public with his work. "I am now looking to write a book on management skills based on my experiences at the workplace," says Sharma.

SHARING THOUGHTS

ASHISH SHARMA'S BOOK *KUCH MOTI DIL KE SAGAR SE* IS A BLEND OF SOME PRICELESS MEMORIES BASED ON HIS PERSONAL LIFE AND EVENTS WHICH AFFECTED HUMANITY

CHARU MALHOTRA

Life is full of incidents which yield precious and everlasting memories to be nurtured throughout the lifetime. When these memories strike, time comes to a halt, and one is taken back to the golden phase. Ashish Sharma's book *Kuch Moti Dil Ke Sagar Se* is a blend of some priceless memories based on his personal life and events which affected humanity on a large scale. It enfolds twenty poems with their English translations.

Savita Bhatti, who launched the book, asserts, "The book comprises poems penned down in simple yet an effective manner so that the readers can easily relate to them. The poems are based on incidents which every person comes across once in their lifetime." She feels that everyone shares similar lives but they pretend to be different in order to prove their superiority. *Kuch Moti Dil Ke Sagar Se*, a Wordit CDE publication, is Ashish's first venture in the literary society with an objective of sharing his thoughts with the readers.

Briefing about the book, he says, "It provides dais to various heart shattering events which have shook the humanity such as 9/11 and 26/11 terrorist attacks; a tribute to Nirbhaya and the missing MH370 incident. It also embraces some excerpts from my personal life". A General Manager at an MNC based in Indonesia, Ashish exclaims, "When I started working on the concept it was never meant to be rolled out to the public. I used to pen down my thoughts whenever I could find some time off from work and finally compile them into poems on weekends." He also shared that he always wanted to become a singer but unfortunately got trapped in the rat race to become an engineer.

When asked about the challenges he faced while working on the book, he answers, "Writing was not an issue but the translation of poems from Hindi to English was quite troublesome because the rhythmic meaning used to fall off-track while the process of translating." Sharma's wife played an important role by helping him in dealing with the challenges. He perceives that people should go for his book as it presents emotions that are common to everyone and moreover the book aims at sharing with the readers some worthy thoughts portrayed simply.

‘कुछ हीरे मन की खान से’ विमोचित

चंडीगढ़, 27 जून (पूजा गोयल): जब हम जिंदगी से थक जाते हैं तो आखिर में ज्ञात होता है की जिसके लिए हम अभी तक भाग रहे थे वह खुशी हमे अंदर से मिलेगी और वह भी लाइफ की छोटी-छोटी चीजों में। कुछ इन्ही सिंपल शब्दों के साथ आशीष शर्मा की किताब ‘कुछ हीरे मन की खान से' का विमोचन किया गया। सविता भट्टी ने इस दौरान कहा कि लाइफ में किसी भी इंसान द्वारा सिंपल चीजों को करना काफी मुश्किल भरा होता है पर वह इसे आसानी से कर देता है।

Echoing Thoughts

ASHISH SHARMA, THE POET FROM CHANDIGARH IS OUT WITH HIS SECOND BOOK TITLED *DIAMONDS FROM THE MINE OF MIND*

GURMEHAR KAUR

"A poet looks at the world the way a man looks at a woman." Wallace Stevens. Boned with ideas and nerved with emotions, it is no wrong to say that the poetry is the skin of emotions. Only the person who dares to realise the reality has the guts to present it to the world through his words.

Ashish Sharma, the poet from Chandigarh who is currently based in Indonesia, is on the same track. We interact with Ashish to have a deeper view to his world of thoughts.

Ashish, who titled his first poetic endeavor as *Pearls from the Ocean of Heart*, has come up with his next book *Diamonds from the Mine of Mind*. "I have tried doing something different with my books. I have written every poem in two languages, Hindi and English.

"It in English the book is titled, *Diamonds from the Mine of Mind*, in Hindi it reads, '*Kuch Heere Mann Ki Khan Se*'," says Ashish.

Working in a IT firm in Indonesia, Ashish says that he developed a taste for writing during his college days. "I started writing when I was pursuing my engineering but always took it as a hobby, and never thought that I will collect and present my poems as a book," he adds.

So, what prompted him to give his thoughts the shape of words, we ask, and he answers, "I was so influenced by the ghazals of Jagjit Singh and also the way Amitabh Bachchan reads the poems of his father, inspired me a lot. So, thoughts were always in my mind and my good thoughts became my poems."

Since, he is new in the world of writing, how tough it was for him to get his book published?

"Honestly, for the first book it was very tough as many of the publishers were not convinced with the English/Hindi concept and I didn't want to change it. But fortunately the publishing head of OpenCrayon.Com liked the concept and both the books got published," he recalls.

The book which took one year to get completed has 20 poems based on different subjects. While describing about the subject of all the poems, Ashish shares, "I always observe things deeply and I have a lot to write. Through this book, I've tried to touch many subjects like social evils and issues, relationships, environment, women empowerment, drug addiction and partition of India-Pakistan among others.

Yogita Sharma, his wife who has translated the poems into English, joins in and says, "Yes the concept is different and readers appreciated the first book. But it is very hard to express the real meaning of emotions in a foreign language, so we've worked hard on that part."

The poet says that he is almost ready with his next book but it will take time to compile the ideas and thoughts. "I don't write to earn money, as I've already achieved a lot in life. I write so that I can convey my thoughts to people and with my words, I want to push them to think once about life and all the other evils around us," he concludes.

A Copy of the books being presented by Ashish to
Hon'ble Ambassador of India to Indonesia & Temor leste
H.E. Mr.Pradeep Kumar Rawat

A Copy of the books being presented by Ashish & Yogita

Former Consul General
of India in Medan
Mr. Basir Ahmed

Former Consul General of India in
Medan Dr. Shalia Shah & her husband
Mr. Prohit Lal

Consul General of Malaysia in Medan
Mr. Amizal Fadzli B. Rajali

Consul General of India in
Medan Mr. Raghu Gururaj

A copy of the books being presented to Mr Manik Paul - winner of India's got talent Season 6

A Copy of the books being presented by Ashish & Yogita

Film Actor & Director Mr. Jasraj Singh Bhatti (Son of Late Sh.Jaspal Bhatti & Madam Savita Bhatti)

The Great Astrologer Sh. P.Khurrana (Father of Bollywood star Mr. Ayushmann Khurrana)

A Copy of the books being presented by Ashish & Yogita

Ms. Deesis Edith Mesiani,
Editor in Chief, Penerbit
Bhuana Ilmu Populer,
Jakarta - Indonesia

Ashish's close friend Brother
Mohamed Hameid Al Sarary
– Director PT. Pacific Indomas
Jakarta, Indonesia

Our Special Thanks to Sister Alice Wijaya & her daughters Winny & Winda
for all their support. You are a family to us.

A Copy of the books being presented by Ashish & Yogita

Director JNICC Dr. Makrand Shukla, Dr. Mrs.Mital Shukla,
Ustad Sh.Shabbir Warsi & Vice Consul at Indian Consulate Medan
Sh.Lawlesh Kumar

Leading journalists in Medan Sister Ranggini Triyono Krisna &
Mela Hapsari

A Copy of the books being presented by Ashish & Yogita

Ashish's close friend
Brother Dr. Abdul Majid

Ms.Sheetal Patil Dalvi
Leading yoga practitioner

My Inspiration - My Family

About the Author

प्रिय पाठकों,

PEARLS from the Ocean of Heart" - ''कुछ मोती दिल के सागर से'' और "DIAMONDS from the Mine of Mind" - ''कुछ हीरे मन की खान से'' को सराहने के लिए शुक्रिया, अब मैं आपके समक्ष, "EMERALDS carved with thoughts" - ''कुछ पन्ने विचारों से तराशे हुए'', प्रस्तुत कर रहा हूँ ।

मेरी पहली दो किताबों की तरह, EMERALDS carved with thoughts"- ''कुछ पन्ने विचारों से तराशे हुए'' भी सभी के लिए अंग्रेजी अनुवाद सहित हिंदी कविताओं का एक अनूठा संग्रह है। ये मेरे जीवन और दुनिया में दिन–ब–दिन होने वाली घटनाओं से प्रेरित हैं। मैने सामाजिक बुराइयों एवं मुद्दों, पर्यावरण, रिश्तों, खुशियों एवं आशाओं और अन्य कई

मुद्दों पर कविता के रूप में अपने विचारों को व्यक्त किया है। मैं बहुत भाग्यशाली हूँ कि इस पुस्तक में मैं कुछ महान हस्तियों, जैसे कि भारत के प्रधानमंत्री आदरणीय श्री नरेंद्र मोदी, भारत के भूतपूर्व प्रधानमंत्री स्वः श्री अटल बिहारी वाजपेयी, सार्थक व्यंग्य के बेताज बादशाह स्वः श्री जसपाल भट्टी, महान परोपकारी और व्यवसायी स्वः श्री हयेल सईद अनाम (HSA) और मेरे आदरणीय माता–पिता प्रोफ. हरिन्दर शर्मा और श्रीमति उत्तरा शर्मा, के सम्मान में लिख पाया हूँ। मैं बड़ी उदारता से गर्व महसूस कर रहा हूँ, कि मैंने दो महान राष्ट्रों - भारत और इंडोनेशिया की 70 साल पुरानी अटूट मित्रता पर भी एक कविता इस पुस्तक में लिखी है। आशा है कि मुझे इस किताब को लिखने मे जितना आनंद आया है आपको इसे पढ़ने में भी उतना ही मजा आएगा। मैं अपनी पत्नी योगिता का, मेरी कविताओं के अंग्रेजी अनुवाद के लिए, आभारी हूँ ।

मैं केवल जुनून के लिए लिखता हूँ, इस लिए मैं सर्वश्रेष्ठ कवियों में शुमार नहीं हो सकता। मैं पंजाब के पटियाला शहर के एक शिक्षाविद परिवार से हूं। मैंने मैकेनिकल इंजीनियरिंग में स्नातक की उपाधि प्राप्त करने के बाद एम.बी.ए किया। उसके बाद मैं काम करने के लिए पिंजौर, हरियाणा चला गया। भारत में तकरीबन सोलह साल कई भारतीय और बहुराष्ट्रीय कंपनियों में काम करने के बाद नवंबर, 2012 में, मैं इंडोनेशिया के मिडान चला आया और फिलहाल मैं मिडान की एक बहुराष्ट्रीय कंपनी में बतौर जनरल मैनेजर कार्यरत हूं। मैं यहां अपनी पत्नी योगिता (मीनू) और अपने प्यारे बेटे अभिलक्ष (लक्षी) के साथ रहता हूं। हमारी प्यारी बिटिया अपूर्वा (अरू) मेलबर्न, आस्ट्रेलिया में उच्च शिक्षा प्राप्त कर रही है।

प्रभु महान हैं, उनका हर क्षण धन्यवाद।

– आशीष शर्मा